Hunting with the Native Americans

ROB STAEGER

Senior Consulting Editor Dr. Troy Johnson
Professor of History and American Indian Studies
California State University

MASON CREST PUBLISHERS • PHILADELPHIA

NATIVE AMERICAN LIFE

NATIVE AMERICAN LIFE

Hunting with the
Native Americans

ROB STAEGER

Senior Consulting Editor Dr. Troy Johnson
Professor of History and American Indian Studies
California State University

MASON CREST PUBLISHERS • PHILADELPHIA

NATIVE AMERICAN LIFE

Dedication: For Nan, with much love. She knew more than anyone how food got on the plate.

Mason Crest Publishers
370 Reed Road
Broomall PA 19008
www.masoncrest.com

14942

First printing

1 3 5 7 9 8 6 4 2

Library of Congress Cataloging-in-Publication Data
on file at the Library of Congress

ISBN 1-59084-127-1

Frontispiece: *The Buffalo Hunt,* a painting by artist Paul Kane.

Table of Contents

Introduction

F or hundreds of years the dominant image of the Native American has been that of a stoic warrior, often wearing a full-length eagle feather headdress, riding a horse in pursuit of the buffalo, or perhaps surrounding some unfortunate wagon train filled with innocent west-bound American settlers. Unfortunately there has been little written or made available to the general public to dispel this erroneous generalization. This misrepresentation has resulted in an image of native people that has been translated into books, movies, and television programs that have done little to look deeply into the native worldview, cosmology, and daily life. Not until the 1990 movie *Dances with Wolves* were native people portrayed as having a human persona. For the first time, native people could express humor, sorrow, love, hate, peace, and warfare. For the first time native people could express themselves in words other than "ugh" or "Yes, Kemo Sabe." This series has been written to provide a more accurate and encompassing journey into the world of the Native Americans.

When studying the native world of the Americas, it is extremely important to understand that there are few "universals" that apply across tribal boundaries. With over 500 nations and 300 language groups the worlds of the Native Americans were diverse. The traditions of one group may or may not have been shared by neighboring groups. Sports, games, dance, subsistence patterns, clothing, and religion differed—greatly in some instances. And although nearly all native groups observed festivals and ceremonies necessary to insure the renewal of their worlds, these too varied greatly.

Of equal importance to the breaking down of old myopic and stereotypic images is that the authors in this series credit Native

Americans with a sense of agency. Contrary to the views held by the Europeans who came to North and South America and established the United States, Canada, Mexico, and other nations, some Native American tribes had sophisticated political and governing structures— that of the member nations of the Iroquois League, for example. Europeans at first denied that native people had religions but rather "worshiped the devil," and demanded that Native Americans abandon their religions for the Christian worldview. The readers of this series will learn that native people had well-established religions, led by both men and women, long before the European invasion began in the 16th and 17th centuries.

Gender roles also come under scrutiny in this series. European settlers in the northeastern area of the present-day United States found it appalling that native women were "treated as drudges" and forced to do the men's work in the agricultural fields. They failed to understand, as the reader will see, that among this group the women owned the fields and scheduled the harvests. Europeans also failed to understand that Iroquois men were diplomats and controlled over one million square miles of fur-trapping area. While Iroquois men sat at the governing council, Iroquois clan matrons caucused with tribal members and told the men how to vote.

These are small examples of the material contained in this important series. The reader is encouraged to use the extended bibliographies provided with each book to expand his or her area of specific interest.

Dr. Troy Johnson
Professor of History and American Indian Studies
California State University

In this canvas from 1832–33, American artist
George Catlin captured the teamwork Plains
Indians needed when hunting buffalo.

1 Teamwork

Hunting is often seen as a struggle between human and animal. A hunter tracks an animal and waits for the prey to come into sight. Only then does the hunter fire. It's a one-on-one conflict, and the hunter almost always comes out the winner.

Before European colonization, hunting in America was quite different. True, hunters sometimes stalked their prey alone. But often, hunting was a group activity. It wasn't enough to kill one deer. Tribes needed much more to keep fed, clothed, and equipped. Native Americans hunted using arrows, clubs, and harpoons, among other tools, but cooperation and teamwork were the most powerful weapons they had.

This teamwork showed in the way people fished. In the Northeast, men built traps out of sticks and nets. The nets stopped the fish, and the men stood in the water and speared them. The trap they built together made the fishing better for everyone.

Deer hunting worked the same way. Men built a long *corral* and drove a herd of deer into the open end of the corral. The deer would find themselves trapped at the far end, where the hunters could kill them using spears and arrows. However, the hunters could not have done it without help. The shouting women, the men who built the

This illustration from a 16th-century French manuscript depicts two Native American hunters carrying a wild boar they have killed.

corral, and the other hunters who chased the deer all played their parts.

The same system was used for hunting buffalo on the Great Plains. It also worked for caribou hunters in the Arctic. In the Southwest and in Central America, animals were surrounded and clubbed to death.

On the northern coast of the Pacific Ocean, tribes like the Nootka and the Tlingit hunted whales. Teamwork made the hunts possible. Whales weigh thousands of pounds. Simply towing one back to shore required cooperation. Hunting one was an intricate process in which everyone had a job to do.

Native hunters of the time would probably agree that teamwork between hunters was critical. However, they would probably say that other forms of cooperation were even more important. For a successful hunt, they believed that the animals had to work with the hunters.

Tribes danced and made offerings to animal spirits before a hunt. The rituals were a message to the animals, asking them to sacrifice themselves for the tribe. If the ritual was performed correctly, the animals would have no choice but to obey and die.

Once the hunt was over, animals were always thanked. Some, like the bear, were honored with feasts and tobacco. Their bodies and their meat were treated with respect. Like the hunters, the **shaman** who blessed the hunt, and the women who butchered the kills, animals had an important part to play as well. The hunt went best when the people and the animals cooperated. In the view of Native American societies, hunting was based on teamwork, and everyone, including the animals, was on the same team. ❦

Inuit villagers in modern-day Alaska butcher a whale. For centuries Native American tribes in the Pacific Northwest and the Far North ventured into the ocean to hunt whales, a rich source of meat and blubber.

11

Fish formed an important part of the diets of many Native American tribes in the Northeast. Here, a trap enables men in a canoe to easily collect large numbers of fish.

2. Hunting in the Northeast

Farming was difficult in the American Northeast. The growing season wasn't long enough to support many crops. Some tribes grew corn, squash, and beans, but these crops were not central to their diet. Most of what they ate came from gathering wild plants, hunting, and fishing.

The Atlantic Ocean was home to many types of fish. Coastal tribes caught herring, smelt, sturgeon, and shad. On the shores of Long Island, tribes like the Montauk dug for clams. Others harvested oysters. People even ate whale meat if one of these giant mammals washed up on shore. No one went to sea to hunt them, however.

Further inland, people fished in freshwater streams and lakes. The Great Lakes were full of trout, whitefish, and sturgeon. Tribes such as the Chippewa and Ojibwa built bark houses on the shores to live in while they fished. Among the Chippewa, women did most of the fishing. Chippewa men ice-fished in the winter and spear-fished in the spring.

Woodland Indians fished in many different ways. Some used hook and line, like some fishermen today. Others caught fish using nets and traps. Some hunters speared fish or shot them with arrows. It was even possible to catch fish by hand. A man simply slipped his hand into the water and kept it completely still. Eventually, a fish nudged against it,

> **Woodland Indians often soaked their fishing nets in a mixture of water and sumac leaves to kill the smell of fish. They believed that fish wouldn't go near a stinky net.**

thinking his hand was just another rock. If the man was quick enough, he could grab the fish and throw it to shore.

Woodland Indians fished with nets called *seines*. Seines are large nets that stretch across a body of water. Some tribes built wooden frames for the nets at the mouths of rivers. When fish swam upriver to *spawn*, they could pass through the frames. Then, men would dive into the water and stretch a long net across the frame. When the fish swam back downstream, the net stopped them. Men speared the fish as they gathered around the trap. Some tribes just scooped them out of the water using baskets.

Traps like this weren't only used in the Northeast. Southeastern and Northwestern tribes used them, too. The point of fish traps was to get the fish to stay in one place. Seines were good for this, but they weren't the only way. Sometimes, people arranged rocks in a V formation, artificially narrowing the river. The V-shape funneled the fish to waiting hunters, who clubbed them and pulled them out.

Algonquian men fished from their canoes using bark-fiber nets. Some used dip nets attached to handheld frames. Others dragged larger nets along as they paddled. Nets made it easy to capture a lot of fish at once. In addition, the catch usually included a wide variety. At night, fishermen held up torches to attract fish. Curious fish were speared and pulled out of the lake.

Spearfishing was one of many methods
Indians devised to take fish.

An Ojibwa snowshoe dance, held after the first snowfall of the season to thank the spirits for their help in a successful hunt.

Some Woodland Indians fished using a hook and a line. They baited a hook made of deer bone with an old piece of blanket. They tied the line around their wrist and wrapped the line around an oar. Then they dropped the hook into the water. The motion of the oars made the bait seem alive.

Winter freezes didn't stop Northeastern fishermen. After cutting a hole in the ice, a fisherman lowered in a wooden *lure*. Lures were carved to look like frogs or minnows. The fisherman would lie flat on his stomach and cover his head with a blanket. This kept any light from seeping into the hole. He would jiggle the lure, hoping to attract a fish and spear it through the hole.

Northeasterners ate much more than fish, however. Wild birds such as turkeys, geese, and heron made their way into the cook pot. Also hunted were moose, beaver, wolves, and foxes. Even bears were sometimes hunted, despite the danger they posed.

Hunters preferred to trap bears instead of fighting them directly. There were two types of traps that worked for bears: pitfalls and deadfalls. A pitfall was a deep pit covered by grass or branches. When the bear stepped onto the branches, they would break, and it would fall into the pit.

Deadfalls worked in a different way. A dead tree or boulder was propped up on a hill. A bear in the target area triggered the trap. The weight would then roll onto the bear, keeping it trapped until the hunter arrived.

17

Both traps needed something to draw the bear in. Honey, apples, and pork worked well. So did berries and beaver musk. Whichever lure was used, a shaman added a second, magic lure to the trap. Most tribes had special ceremonies for bear hunts. The magic lure was part of that.

Hunters had many other rituals as well. Before a hunt, they *fasted* and made sacrifices. They often asked guardian spirits for help. Some even cut

People treated bears with great respect. They called the bear "Grandfather" or "Grandmother." Often, hunters put a pipe of tobacco between the dead bear's teeth as a thank-you gift for its sacrifice.

THE USES OF DEER

Hunting deer was important to Indian society in the East. Deer flesh provided a great deal of meat, but that was only the beginning. Their hides were tanned into soft leather, which was used for clothing, moccasins, bags, arrow cases, pouches—even thongs for lacrosse sticks.

Deer-bone knives were common, and the bone was used in other tools as well. Although bows were normally made of wood, it was possible to make one almost entirely from deer. Antlers were sometimes tied together with leather thongs and made into bows. Deer tendons were used as bowstrings. If need be, the animal's bones were chipped into arrowheads. Only the shaft of the arrow had to be wood.

their own flesh, which showed respect for the animals' suffering.

Another ritual was the Ojibwa tribe's snowshoe dance, which celebrated the first snowfall of the year. Snow made hunting easier in many ways. Animal tracks were clearer in fresh snow, for example. Also, animals sometimes trapped themselves in snowdrifts. The dance thanked the spirits for the help they were giving.

Winter was a good time for trapping as well. Hunters set traps along animal paths. The traps caught smaller animals, such as lynx, beavers, and partridges. Each day, hunters checked their traps and removed any caught animals. The snow made it easy to see the paths animals favored.

The main prey of the Woodland Indians was the white-tailed deer. Countless native tools and clothing came from the deer, as did a generous amount of meat. To attract deer, some tribes set fire to parts of the forest each spring. The new grass that grew after the fire brought deer and other grazing animals, which made them easier to hunt.

Hunting was done using spears or bows and arrows. Hunters imitated the sounds deer made to lure them into striking distance. Rubbing antlers together sounded like two male deer in a fight. Imitating a fawn attracted deer, but it could also cause problems. Sometimes the hunter came face-to-face with a wildcat or wolf looking to attack a helpless fawn. Hunters had to be ready for unexpected guests.

Another way to catch deer off-guard was by distracting them. Bright lights usually dazzle deer, leaving them stunned. So hunters would set up torches on a platform in a lake. When a deer came to drink, it would see the torches and freeze. Hunters would then shoot the deer with arrows before it could move.

19

Deer hunters also banded together to hunt deer in large drives. Deer drives were something that Woodland Indians had in common with the tribes of the Southeast. ⑤

Native Americans perform a bear dance. The Creek Indians of the Southeast held a large feast every time they managed to kill a bear.

3 Hunting in the Southeast

In the 16th and 17th centuries, the Powhatan tribes were one of the most prominent groups in Virginia. Led by Chief Powhatan, they banded together in the late 1500s. Like many groups in the region, the Powhatans were primarily farmers. Still, fish and *game* were an important part of their diet. In the Virginia tidewater area, most of the food came from the sea. Women tended the fields, growing corn, squash, tobacco, and other crops. Men fished and sometimes hunted to feed their families.

As in the North, men fished using nets, fishing line, or bows. When fishing, archers tied a cord to their arrows. That way, they could pull the fish aboard their canoe.

Further inland, men fished from rivers. Creek Indians used traps, nets, and fishing lines with turkey-bone hooks. Their fishing spears were tipped with the jagged tails of horseshoe crabs.

Sometimes, Creek fishermen poisoned their own streams. They ground a poisonous root called "devil's horseshoe" into powder and mixed it into the water. Devil's horseshoe was a narcotic. It paralyzed fish as they swam without making their meat poisonous. The fish floated to the surface and were easy to collect with nets.

On the coast, men hunted small game. Raccoons, foxes, squirrels, beavers, rabbits, and wild turkeys were all common catches. Hunters often used

Some areas didn't have stone suitable for arrowheads. In those cases, hunters tipped their arrows with sharpened deer bones, antlers, or even bird beaks.

snares rather than stalking their prey. To set a snare, a hunter tied a noose using a cord made of plant fiber. He attached it to a sapling, or young tree, near an animal path. He bent the tree close to the ground and secured it there. Then he hid the noose under a layer of leaves. When a raccoon or other small animal stepped into the noose, it triggered the trap. The tree would straighten, pulling the noose tight around the raccoon's paw and lifting it into the air.

The hunter would find the raccoon when he checked his traps. He'd cut the raccoon down, kill it, and reset the trap. Hunters set a number of traps in an area. They checked their traps each day to see what they caught.

In Louisiana, hunters used *bolas* to snag ducks and birds. A bola consisted of three weights attached to cords made of animal *sinew*. Hunters threw bolas to hit birds in flight.

Other Southern Indians hunted water birds in lakes. They waited underwater, breathing through hollow reeds. When birds landed, they leaped up to grab them.

Further inland, the game grew bigger. Deer and bear were more common. Some tribes didn't eat bear, hunting them only for their fat

This illustration depicts Native Americans hunting beavers with bows and arrows and muskets obtained in trade with whites. Some tribes in the East and Southeast included beaver meat as part of their traditional diet, but as more whites settled in North America, beavers became prized mainly for their pelts, which were a valuable trading item.

In 1657, a Powhatan tribe was accused of shooting an English colonist's pigs. The farmer had *branded* his pigs and let them run freely until he needed them. The tribe's leader, called a *werowance*, defended his people. He argued that the English had been shooting his deer, so it was only fair that the Powhatans shot the colonist's pigs.

The English man argued that he hadn't shot any deer with tribal markings. The werowance said, "Indeed, none of my deer are marked, and by that you may know them to be mine; and when you meet with any that are marked, you may do as you please, for they are none of mine."

and fur. Others, like the Creek, held big feasts whenever they killed a bear. They would lay out a set of clothes and some of the bear's favorite food to thank it for providing the meal.

Often, men hunted deer alone. They carried bows and dressed in deerskins to disguise their scent and camouflage them, allowing them to creep closer to unsuspecting deer.

When deer were in large numbers, hunters worked together. The way to catch the most deer in the shortest time was a drive. Deer drives were common across the eastern part of the continent, in the North and South alike. Drives took the effort of the entire community. Men chopped down trees and arranged them into a V-shaped corral. At one end, the corral was wide and open. It was easy for deer to step inside without realizing it. The corral gradually narrowed to a point. There was no opening at the narrow end; deer that ran into it found a dead end.

Once the corral was built, hunters needed to herd the deer into it. Usually, they frightened the deer into moving. Hunters howled like wolves or banged animal bones together. Many tribes chased the deer with dogs. People sometimes even lit forest fires to drive the deer out of the woods. Anything was possible, as long as it got the deer into the mouth of the V.

Once the deer entered, they were funneled into the point. There, hunters waited with spears. When the deer arrived, they could kill them all in one place. In a sense, this way of hunting was not much different from the traps used for fish.

Sometimes, the corral funneled deer into a lake or river. In that case, men would be waiting in boats. The swimming deer made easy targets for the hunters.

There was a reason Native Americans devised these massive killing schemes. It took a great deal of meat to keep a tribe going. A drive provided that meat all at once. Usually, there was enough food to save for later. To preserve a catch, people dried the meat into **jerky**. Meat could also be mashed and seasoned to make **pemmican**. Both stayed edible much longer than fresh meat.

Since hunting was so important to the community, boys started learning when they were young. Fathers trained their sons to shoot at moving targets. The father might throw sticks in the air, and his son

Native Americans take surplus fruit and vegetables to a village storehouse in this 1591 engraving. The storehouse is located along a riverbank so that its contents will stay cool. In the colder climate of the Northeast, tribes dug cache pits to store the extra food they gathered during the summer months.

would fire arrows at them. The boy wouldn't be allowed to eat breakfast until he hit one. If a boy showed unusual daring or skill during the hunt, he might be honored with a new name.

In the 1600s, permanent European settlements began taking hold in Virginia. Many of the new arrivals raised livestock, which created a problem. The colonists left their animals unguarded and unfenced, which made them easy prey for wolves. So colonists hired local tribesmen to hunt the wolves for them. For a while, it worked out well for both sides. The native hunters kept the wolves at bay. In return, they received goods from the colonists. ⑤

Hunting animals as large as the buffalo was an especially
dangerous undertaking. In this detail from a painting by the
renowned Western artist Frederic Remington, a Plains Indian
and his horse meet with disaster in the midst of a stampede.

Hunting in the Great Plains and the Southwest

Throughout the Great Plains, hunting provided the main source of food. There was plenty of game to choose from. Elk, deer, and antelope all roamed the land in great herds. Smaller game, such as rabbits and quail, were also plentiful. However, the most prized animal, by far, was the buffalo. Buffalo provided food, clothing, tools, hides for shelter, and much more. In fact, the buffalo was at the center of Plains culture, and it all began with the hunt.

Most of the year, tribes split into smaller bands. Each hunting band consisted of 20 or 30 families connected by marriage. They moved from camp to camp, hunting elk, antelope, or small game. They carried everything on their backs or on the backs of their dogs, using special A-framed racks called *travois*.

A few times a year, the bands would come together for a buffalo drive. First, people would pray for a good hunt. Then the fastest men would scout for buffalo. When they found a herd, they would send word to the chief. The entire camp would set out for the hunt. Men carried their weapons and hunting bundles. Women brought empty travois. Everyone moved in silence. They approached the herd from downwind so the buffalo couldn't smell them.

> **Young men were offered the tongue of the first buffalo they killed. It was considered the tastiest part. However, it was a custom to give the tongue away to show generosity.**

When they were in position, the women would stand their travois up to make a curved fence. Then, some men would creep upwind of the buffalo. Suddenly, they would shout and howl. The noise would cause the herd to stampede toward the fence. At the fence, other hunters closed in. They shot arrows and threw spears and jabbed at the buffalo with *lances*. All the while, dogs barked and women shouted, hoping to confuse and distract the buffalo.

After the hunt was over, the chief would count the dead animals. Each hunter had his own personal design on his arrows, so it was easy to determine who had killed which animals. The chief divided the meat equally between each family, but he awarded hides according to skill. Once the hides were divided, women began butchering the animals. One exception to this was the Cheyenne. Cheyenne men butchered their own kills.

As winter came, the buffalo headed into the woods. At that point, the men changed their corral-hunting technique. They chopped down trees to make a three-sided corral on the slope of a hill. Inside the corral, they set up sharp stakes at angles. Any buffalo that tried to escape would stab itself. The hunters laid poles smeared with manure and water on the corral floor. When the poles froze, they would be too slippery to move on.

When the corral was finished, a shaman stayed in his lodge, praying that the spirits would make the hunt go well. Although the shaman did

Native hunters disguised in wolf skins
approach a herd of buffalo in this painting
by George Catlin.

A buffalo hunt in late winter. Note that the hunters are on foot. When Europeans brought horses to North America, the way Plains Indians hunted would dramatically change.

not actually hunt with the men, he was recognized as having an important role in the hunt and received his share of the kill.

Nothing changed life on the Great Plains more than the horse. In the middle of the 17th century, horses that had escaped, or been stolen

from, Spanish colonists became common among the tribes. Horses made tribal movement quicker. Tribes could cover 10 times the ground they used to. This led to easier hunting, but also to more intertribal feuds. Suddenly, everyone wanted to hunt on the same land.

Horses not only changed where people hunted, they also changed how people hunted. Buffalo scouts used the horse to send signals to the camp. One signal was to ride a horse in a zigzag pattern within sight of the others. The pattern indicated the herd's size, distance, and direction. Once they got the signal, hunters put away most of their gear. Riders needed to travel light.

A mounted hunter chases a buffalo into an ambush
set up by two other members of the hunting group.
Plains Indians gave equal shares of meat to each
family involved in a hunt, but individuals who
actually killed the animals were awarded their hides.

Riders galloped into the herd and speared buffalo using lances. A single rider could kill three or four as his horse darted between them. However, this was a dangerous stunt. If the horse tripped or the rider fell, the hunter would usually be trampled to death.

> **Many Plains Indians wouldn't eat wild turkey. They believed that turkey meat turned men into cowards.**

A good buffalo-hunting horse was a family's prized possession. These horses were called "buffalo runners." They had to be smart and fast, with great endurance.

Women followed the hunt with packhorses. These horses were trained and bred for strength. Only packhorses could carry the heavy loads of buffalo back to camp.

Horses strengthened tribes like the Sioux, Comanche, and Blackfoot, who had already focused on hunting. By contrast, agricultural tribes, such as the Mandan, Hidatsa, and Arikara, grew less powerful. Other tribes, including the Crow and Cheyenne, turned from farming to hunting when they saw the economic advantage provided by these animals.

Strangely, the horse had a greater effect on hunting than the gun. Native Americans began getting firearms from colonists and other tribes in the late 1600s. However, guns were too noisy for good hunting. A loud gunshot scattered all the other animals in the area. The bow and arrow were silent and, in the hands of a skilled hunter, just as deadly.

Unlike the hunters of the Great Plains, tribes in the Southwest focused on farming. However, it wasn't always that way. Before recorded

35

NATIVE AMERICAN LIFE

history, the Southwestern climate was wetter than it is today. People hunted herds of antelope, deer, and elk. They stalked bighorn sheep in the highlands.

Archaeologists have found collections of twigs twisted to represent animal shapes in Southwestern caves. They may have been charms to communicate with animal spirits and make the hunt go better.

Around 1500 B.C., the *nomadic* hunters began to settle on permanent lands. This opened the door for farming, but it didn't stop hunters. The Hohokam people, who flourished around A.D. 500, hunted using bows and arrows. They painted hunting scenes on rocks that survive to this day.

Around A.D. 1150, the Southwestern climate became much drier, and the animal population thinned. Pueblo tribes, such as the Pima and Papago, began relying more on farming than on hunting for food. Still, hunting didn't disappear entirely.

The winter was the Pueblo tribes' hunting season. Almost everyone took part. Men, women, and children snared small game in woven nets. They hunted rabbits, squirrels, mice, quail, and doves. People surrounded the animals and killed them by throwing rocks and clubs. Originally, animals were rounded up on foot. Later, hunters on horseback drove them together.

Around the 13th century, the Apache and Navajo tribes entered the area from the north. Both tribes were nomadic hunters. The new environment changed Navajo culture dramatically. The Pueblo tribes helped them adapt to the land and begin farming. Eventually, the Navajo began raising domestic animals—in particular, sheep.

Apaches, on the other hand, continued hunting in a land that wasn't well suited for it. However, they survived by becoming extremely good at hunting despite the harsh conditions. Apache men hunted deer and antelope using lances and bows. Boys picked up a bow at a very young age. Before they were ready to hunt with the men, boys hunted small game using slings and rocks.

In the 1600s, things changed. The Apache tribe, and many others, stole horses brought by Spanish missionaries. The horses allowed them to expand their hunting territory. One tribe, the Lipan Apache, even rode their horses to the Great Plains to hunt buffalo. ⑤

37

A modern Inuit fisherman inspects his nets from a kayak. In the Far North, which is too cold for farming, native peoples survived by fishing, venturing into the icy seas to hunt large mammals such as whales, and killing land animals such as caribou.

5 Hunting in the Northwest and Far North

Farming is impossible in the frozen North. The Inuit people could gather some wild plants, but very little grew in the Arctic. People ate mostly meat and fat. Nearly everything they had, from food to clothing to tools, came from animals.

Like other native cultures, the Inuit had great respect for the animals they hunted. They showed their respect with rituals. For example, after killing a seal or walrus, hunters offered it a drink of water. When a woman butchered a caribou, she couldn't break its bones. Inuit tradition also said that it was wrong to cook land creatures and sea creatures in the same pot.

Tribes split into small bands to hunt caribou each summer. Caribou were essential to Inuit life. Their hides were used for clothing and insulation. Spears, harpoons, and sleds were made from antlers and bones. Caribou sinew was used for thread.

Inuit hunters and fishermen shared their catches with the entire band. This cooperation was essential. Without it, a simple run of bad luck could kill an entire family. Instead, hardship, as well as good fortune, was spread out evenly.

As in the East, the most effective hunting was cooperative. Caribou drives in the North were as common as deer drives in the East. Men built corral walls out of dirt, stone, or even snow. Sometimes, they turned stones upright to form the walls of the V. These stones scared caribou, which may have mistook them for hunters. The upturned stones were called *inukhuit*, or "likenesses of men."

With shouts and barking dogs, men drove the caribou to a place where hunters waited to kill them. Sometimes, it was the end of the corral. In other cases the animals might be driven over a cliff, which killed most of them immediately. Often, they were driven into a river or lake, where hunters waited in enclosed, one-man boats called kayaks. Their spears were attached to the kayak within easy reach. When the caribou hit the water, the hunters were ready. The awkward, paddling beasts were no match for the hunters' swift boats.

Coastal tribes also used kayaks to hunt seals. Land-based seal hunters used camouflage. They wore wooden helmets carved to look like seals' heads and slid through puddles trying to act like seals. However, they were always ready to throw their spears whenever a real seal came close.

Seals weren't even safe below the ice. Clever hunters looked for the breathing holes seals used. They hung a feather over the hole in the ice. When it moved, the hunter knew a seal was using the hole to breathe. Without hesitation, the hunter would drive a spear through the ice and into the seal. Once the seal was dead, he would chop a hole in the ice and haul the animal out.

Probably the most dangerous animal the Inuit hunted was the polar bear. Once scouts spotted a polar bear, they returned and told their group. Next, the hunters took a position on the ice, keeping themselves

Waiting at a seal's breathing hole in the ice is a time-
tested Inuit method of hunting these sea mammals.

41

Two native hunters with their prey in northern Canada. Today, many native groups preserve the traditions of their ancestors, which required that an animal's spirit be honored after a successful hunt.

between the bear and the ocean. This blocked the bear's path of escape.

When the men were in place, they sent dogs to surround the bear. Then the men approached. They stayed behind the dogs and jabbed long spears at the bear. The man who landed the killing blow was awarded half of the bearskin, but everyone shared its meat.

The best place to hunt polar bears was on the vast sheets of ice attached to the land. However, it was slippery, dangerous work. For one thing, a bear could kill a man in an instant. In addition, the icy surface was almost as deadly as the bear itself. Ice *floes* could break off from the land at any moment. If a hunter was caught on one, he was stuck. Swimming through the freezing water would kill him. His only hope was to hunt seals until the ice drifted back to land. Sometimes, it never did.

In addition to seal, caribou, and bear, the Inuit hunted wolves. Hunters used pitfalls, deadfalls, and box traps to catch them. Two other methods were especially gruesome but effective. One was to imbed sharp splinters of caribou bone into ice and then smear the ice with blood and fat. When a wolf came to lick the ice, it would cut its tongue. When it tasted its own fresh blood, instinct would kick in. The wolf would continue to lick, even though it would slash its tongue worse every time, and slowly bleed to death.

43

Another way to hunt wolves was to freeze a coiled-up caribou bone in a ball of fat. Wolves would eat the frozen ball. Soon, their stomachs would melt the fat, and the sharp bone would uncoil. It was only a matter of time before the wolf died from internal bleeding.

Birds provided another source of food. They were hunted with nets, bows and arrows, and bolas. Some hunters placed nooses under the surface of shallow lakes, pulling them shut if a goose or duck stepped into it. In the winter, people baited the roofs of their snow houses. When

It took at least 150 caribou to feed an Inuit family and its dogs for a year.

a bird landed, the hunter would grab it through a hole. He could get a meal without even leaving his house!

Fish also had a place in the Inuit diet. If the caribou hunt had gone well, they could eat stored food until it came time to hunt seal. However, more often than not, there was a lean time between the hunts. Ice fishing kept people from starving.

Certain rituals were observed when ice fishing. For example, it was considered bad luck to spill water beforehand. Also, men placed the fish they caught in a circle around the fishing hole and always pointed their heads inward. This encouraged other fish to swim near.

Whales were an important source of meat, blubber, and oil. Their *baleen* was also useful. Baleen is a flexible growth in certain kinds of whales' mouths. Indians would make it into fishing lines, nets, and other useful items.

Whales were hunted farther down the Pacific coast as well. The Nootka people were excellent whale hunters. Hunting the California gray whale, which could weigh up to 40 tons, was a strenuous task. Nootka hunters prepared themselves physically and spiritually. For months before the hunt, the Nootka chief took icy baths during the waxing moon. Also, he stopped eating land animals. A few nights before the hunt, the other whalers joined him in the rituals.

The night before the hunt, men painted their faces black, stripped, and carried their open boats, called umiaks, to shore. They poisoned the tips of their spears with *aconitine*. The hunt began at dawn. With the chief's boat in the lead, the hunters approached the whale in single file. They kept behind it, out of its field of vision. Once the whale was in range, the chief hurled his harpoon. Then the other men threw their harpoons.

When the whale dove, men scrambled to let out their harpoon lines. The lines had sealskin floats, called *avatuks*, attached every 50 feet. The floats showed the hunters where the whale was while it was underwater. When it resurfaced, the hunters renewed their attack. They couldn't let the whale catch its breath.

Eventually, the whale would tire and float to the surface to

WOMEN AND THE HUNT

The men of the Arctic had the dangerous job of hunting. They put their lives on the line to feed their families. It was the women's job to keep them safe during the hunt. Women did this by performing rituals. For example, women wore their parkas inside their homes to keep their husbands from freezing.

During a whale hunt, the chief's wife would lie still in their bed. It was believed this kept the boats and the hunters safe from storms and from the whales themselves.

Sometimes, men didn't come back from a hunt. When this happened, women would hang a pair of boots on a hook. The direction and manner in which the boots hung indicated where a woman's husband was. The woman would only give up hope if he didn't return by the start of the next hunting season.

Native American hunters in a canoe close in on a moose. A popular hunting technique among some Indian tribes was to chase large animals into a body of water, where fellow hunters awaited. Not only was a swimming moose, elk, or deer slower, it was also less dangerous.

die. As the hunters towed the dead whale toward shore, they promised to honor it. The chief's wife met it on shore and thanked the whale's spirit for its sacrifice.

Hunting was seasonal in the Pacific Northwest. From February to April, men hunted fur seals. They turned to sea otters in spring. In the summer, they would hunt sea lions and whales. Harbor seals and dolphins would also be in season.

Some tribes crossed the Rocky Mountains for food. When horses became common in the 1700s, the Nez Percé crossed the Rockies each year to hunt bison. The Northern Shoshone did the same.

> Spokane Indians wouldn't eat black bear meat in May or July. Bears ate red ant nests and skunk cabbage in those months, which made their meat taste funny.

From May to September, salmon rushed up the rivers, keeping fishermen busy. Tribal life revolved around the salmon running upstream. Many Northwestern tribes made camp near the Columbia and Fraser Rivers. The Sanpoil and Nespelem tribes built platforms in the middle of the rivers. When the fish returned downstream, hunters speared fish by the dozen.

Fishermen in the region used a variety of nets. Gill nets were designed so that fish could stick only their heads through the holes. When the fish tried to back out, it would catch its gills on the twine.

Reef nets were larger. The bottom of a reef net was anchored to the river floor. The top of it was strung between two canoes. Salmon would swim into the net and be caught by the men in the canoes.

Other nets acted as funnels. Fish swam through a big funnel net into a smaller area. There, men in canoes would catch them using handheld nets.

In the fall, women took over the salmon harvest. Men turned to hunting deer, caribou, and elk. Boys hunted snakes, lizards, and even grasshoppers. This taught them to hunt so they would be ready for larger game by the time they were men. ⑤

47

A descendant of the Mayans, who flourished in
Central America before the arrival of Columbus, fishes
in a river in modern-day Belize. The Mayans relied
mostly on farming, but they also fished and hunted
small game.

6 Hunting in Central and South America

The Indians of Central and South America are better known for their empires than for their individual tribes. Maya, Aztec, and Inca societies were complex and multilayered. Most people who lived in their vast cities never hunted at all. There was little reason to. Farming and butchering domesticated animals met most of their food needs. It was a system close to the life we lead today, in which very little of the food we eat comes from the wild.

The Mayans formed one of the first great civilizations in southern Mexico and Central America. Before the Mayans came to power, the people in the area were fishermen. The men hunted turtles from dugout canoes. Women and children pulled **mollusks** out of the riverbank mud. Most other game was hunted by getting dogs to chase prey into waiting nets.

Although most Mayans never hunted, some caught birds for sacrifices or decoration. They carved special bird bolts out of wood. The bolts were arrows that could take a bird down without damaging its feathers.

When the Aztecs came to power in Mexico in the 1300s, men still hunted on the outskirts of their cities. They stalked and shot deer or lured them using decoy whistles. Hunters sold deer and rabbit hides to city dwellers. Aztec fishermen used traps and nets to catch fish.

Birds were an important source of food in the villages. From October to March, ducks and geese migrated to Aztec territory. Hunters knocked them to the ground with curved clubs. Sometimes they crept up on the birds as they roosted. They would hang nets in the trees and then startle the birds. When the frightened birds took off, some flew into the nets.

Another trick to hunting birds was to hang a sticky plant in a popular clearing. When birds landed to feed, some would get stuck to the plant. Birds such as quail and pigeons stayed in the area year-round. Rich people passed the time by hunting them with blowguns.

The Incas of South America also considered hunting a sport. Incan emperors organized royal hunts for entertainment. Thousands of people would gather in a large circle in the wilderness. They shouted and beat the grass. This drove animals to the center of the giant circle. As the circle got smaller, people threw bolas to catch the animals. They killed any male animals. Female animals were set free. Afterward, the emperor would hold a feast. Uneaten food would be put into the city's reserves.

Aside from the royal hunts, Incas needed a license to hunt legally. In some seasons, people automatically had a license. At other times, the emperor's staff only granted a small number of them.

One tribe not associated with these empires was the Jivaro. The Jivaro live today in the jungles of Ecuador. They were one of the only tribes that successfully resisted conquest when encountered by the Spanish.

Unlike many city dwellers of earlier times, Jivaro hunters are very much aware of the importance of hunting. The food a Jivaro hunter brings home feeds his own family. Jivaro men usually hunt within a few

Mounted South American hunters swing their bolas while chasing a rhea, a large flightless bird similar to an ostrich. The bola was a thrown snaring weapon made from stones and cords.

Jivaro hunters of the South American rain forest shoot their traditional weapon, the blowgun. Simple yet fearsome, the blowgun consists of a hollow tube into which the hunter places a dart tipped with curare, a powerful poison that quickly paralyzes prey.

miles of their homes. A hunter generally goes out alone or with one of his wives. She prepares food for her husband and takes care of the dog.

> The biggest royal hunt on record was organized in 1536 by the emperor Manco Inca. Ten thousand people made up the circle, which ran almost 50 miles around.

Jivaro men make their own blowguns from the hollow stems of palm leaves, which grow up to seven feet long. The darts inside them are poisoned with *curare*, a deadly muscle toxin. They use the blowguns to hunt monkeys, toucans, and even anacondas. Hunters sometimes bring rifles as well. These are the result of trade with other tribes or contact with white men.

Jivaro men fish barehanded or with a hook and line. Occasionally, they poison a river and collect the fish that rise to the surface.

Hunting is also crucial to a young Jivaro boy's passage to adulthood. Teens go into the jungle alone to stalk and kill a tree sloth. They have to chop off its head and make it into a *tsantsa*, or a shrunken head. When finished, the young man returns home to a big party.

Another tribe, the Yanomamo, was not even known to the outside world until the second half of the 20th century. The Yanomamo live in Venezuela in villages along the banks of the Orinoco River.

To hunt, Yanomamo villages break into camps of 30 to 40 people. In their camps, they live mostly on wild food. Women bring some *plantains* from their home gardens in case the hunting isn't good.

53

NATIVE AMERICAN LIFE

The Yanomamo hunt game birds similar to pheasant and turkey called marashi and paruri. Hunters leave their villages before sunrise to catch the birds before they awake. They also hunt wild pigs, alligators, spider monkeys, tapirs, and deer. In some areas, it is necessary to hunt large snakes, but they're not considered good food. The same is true of toads and frogs.

One staple of the Yanomamo diet is the palm grub. These are fat, soft insects that eat dead palm trees. To attract them, Yanomamo men cut down a palm tree. A few days later, they return to it with digging sticks. The men use the sticks to dig the grubs out of the tree. If a grub is damaged, the digger will eat it right there. Otherwise, they're brought back to the village and cooked on a fire. The bugs are so fatty that they crackle like bacon.

One of the most interesting Yanomamo hunting practices is the armadillo hunt. Armadillos live in underground burrows, each of which has several escape tunnels. The burrows protect the armadillo from being hunted in the usual way, so the Yanomamo devised a more creative way to catch them. When a hunter finds an armadillo's escape tunnel, he lights a fire next to it. He uses old termite nests, which create a lot of smoke and burn for a long time. Once the fire is going, the hunter fans smoke into the tunnel.

Soon, the burrow is filled with smoke. Then it is easy to spot the other tunnels as smoke rises from them. As soon as the tunnels are found, other men fill them in with dirt.

Then, they kneel down between the exits and put their ears to the ground. Eventually, a hunter will hear frantic digging down below. The armadillo is trying to escape. The men all begin digging over the spot. About two or three feet down, they'll find the armadillo. By the time they reach it, it is usually dead from smoke inhalation.

The Yanomamo armadillo hunt is a modern example of the teamwork used by most Native American hunters throughout history. Any group that depends on hunting needs cooperation to survive. Without teamwork, the armadillo would be safe in its tunnels and the Yanomamo would go home hungry. Teamwork, a weapon of awesome power, has usually been more than a match for any animal's defenses. ⑤

Chronology

400 B.C. Mayan civilization begins.

12th century A.D. Incas establish capital at Cuzco.

1325 Aztecs found their capital city, Tenochtitlán.

1492 Christopher Columbus sails to America in search of a shorter route to the Far East.

1521 Spanish capture Tenochtitlán, conquering the Aztecs.

1524 Spanish capture Mayan city of Chichen Itza.

1532 Spanish conquer Incas.

1536 Manco Inca, an Incan emperor chosen by the Spanish, stages an enormous royal hunt.

1570 Thirty different Virginia tribes join together under Chief Powhatan.

1620 Pilgrims settle at Plymouth, Massachusetts.

1651 Virginia settlers begin hiring Native Americans to hunt wolves for them.

1670 Guns first traded to Native Americans on Hudson Bay.

Late 1600s Plains Indians begin to get horses.

mid-1700s Horses become widespread among Plains Indians.

1804 U.S. government enacts Louisiana Territory Act, which tries to move Southeastern Indians west of the Mississippi River.

1812 War of 1812 begins; most Indians side with the British.

1813–1814 The Creeks declare war on the United States, resulting in the loss of 22 million acres to the U.S. government.

1830   Congress passes the Indian Removal Act, calling for Native Americans living east of the Mississippi River to be moved to a government-established Indian Territory located in what is present-day Oklahoma.

1838   Cherokee are forced to move from the Southeast to Oklahoma on the "Trail of Tears."

1867   United States buys Alaska.

1887   The Dawes/General Allotment Act divides reservations into 80- and 160-acre tracts; these land parcels are to be owned by individual Indians.

1952   The Federal Relocation Policy is passed; this policy seeks to terminate all government services for Native Americans, negate treaty agreements, and relocate Native Americans from reservations to inner cities.

1971   Congress passes the Alaska Native Claims Settlement Act.

1972   "Trail of Broken Treaties" organized by AIM results in a weeklong occupation of the Bureau of Indian Affairs headquarters in Washington, D.C.

1992   This year marks the 500th anniversary of Columbus' entry to the West Indies, prompting many Native American artists to create artwork expressing their feelings about Columbus and subsequent Europeans and their effects upon the Native American culture.

2003   Recent census estimates indicate there are more than 3 million Native Americans living in the United States and Canada

Glossary

aconitine a poisonous herb used in the Pacific Northwest for whaling.

baleen a flexible growth in whales' mouths, used for making nets and fishing line.

bola a thrown snaring weapon made of stones and cords.

brand a mark made by burning with a hot iron to indicate ownership.

corral a pen or enclosure for capturing wild animals or holding livestock.

curare a deadly muscle toxin.

fast to go without food for a period of time.

floe a usually large, flat, free-floating mass of sea ice.

game wild animals hunted for sport or food.

jerky meat dried for preservation.

lance a sharp, spearlike object.

lure artificial bait used for catching fish.

mollusk any of several varieties of shellfish.

nomadic roaming about from place to place.

pemmican pulverized meat, mashed with berries.

plantain a fruit similar in shape and texture to a banana.

seine a large net that stretches across and extends to the bottom of a body of water.

shaman a spiritual leader of a community with powers gained through mystical visions; also called medicine man.

sinew animal tendons.

snare a device often consisting of a noose for entangling birds or mammals.

spawn to produce or deposit eggs.

travois a wooden frame shaped like an *A;* Plains Indians fitted dogs with them to carry items.

Further Reading

Billard, Jules B., ed. *The World of the American Indian.* Washington, D.C.:
National Geographic Society, 1974.

Carew-Miller, Anna. *Native American Cooking.* Philadelphia: Mason Crest
Publishers, 2003.

Chagnon, Napoleon A. *Yanomamo: The Fierce People.* New York: Holt, Rinehart
and Winston, 1983.

Feest, Christian F. *The Powhatan Tribes.* Philadelphia: Chelsea House
Publishers, 1990.

Franklin, Paula A. *Indians of North America.* New York: David McKay Company,
Inc., 1979.

Kendall, Ann. *Everyday Life of the Incas.* New York: Dorset Press, 1973.

Moulton, Candy. *Everyday Life Among the American Indians.* Cincinnati:
Writer's Digest Books, 2001.

Ritzenthaler, Robert E., and Pat Ritzenthaler. *The Woodland Indians.* Garden
City, N.Y.: Natural History Press, 1979.

Stuart, George E., and Gene S. Stuart. *The Mysterious Maya.* Washington, D.C.:
National Geographic Society, 1977.

Waldman, Carl. *Atlas of the North American Indian.* New York: Facts on File
Publications, 1985.

Internet Resources

http://www.kstrom.net/isk/mainmenu.html
This Web site contains extensive resource material on Native Americans.

http://www.uwgb.edu/galta/mrr/jivaro/
This site contains a wealth of information on the culture, rituals, and history of the Jivaro Indians.

http://members.tripod.com/~PHILKON/
This site lists more than 3,000 historical events that happened to or affected the native peoples of North America.

http://www.channel-e-philadelphia.com/nattopics.html
The Native American Timeline Web site includes time frames, topics, resources, and a discussion forum for all sorts of information pertaining to Native Americans.

http://www.nativeweb.org/resources/
This Web site features a collection of resources and links to informative Native American Web sites.

http://www.si.edu/resource/faq/nmai/start.htm
This site contains fascinating information collected by the Smithsonian Institution about Native American history and culture.

http://www.ilt.columbia.edu/k12/naha/natime.html
This is a timeline of Native American history and includes information on various events.

www.nativepeoples.com
This is the Web site for *Native People's Arts and Lifeways* magazine. It contains information on all sorts of issues pertaining to native peoples.

NATIVE AMERICAN LIFE

Index

Picture Credits

NATIVE AMERICAN LIFE

Contributors

Dr. Troy Johnson is a Professor of American Indian Studies and History at California State University, Long Beach, California. He is an internationally published author and is the author, co-author, or editor of fifteen books, including *Contemporary Political Issues of the American Indian* (1999), *Red Power: The American Indians' Fight for Freedom* (1999), *American Indian Activism: Alcatraz to the Longest Walk* (1997), and *The Occupation of Alcatraz Island: Indian Self-Determination and the Rise of Indian Activism* (1996). He has published numerous scholarly articles, has spoken at conferences across the United States, and is a member of the editorial board of the journals *American Indian Culture and Research* and *The History Teacher.* Dr. Johnson has served as president of the Society of History Education since 2001. He has been profiled in *Reference Encyclopedia of the American Indian* (2000) and *Directory of American Scholars* (2000). He has won awards for his permanent exhibit at Alcatraz Island; he also was named Most Valuable Professor of the Year by California State University, Long Beach, in 1997. He served as associate director and historical consultant on the PBS documentary film *Alcatraz Is Not an Island* (1999), which won first prize at the 26th annual American Indian Film Festival and was screened at the Sundance Film Festival in 2001. Dr. Johnson lives in Long Beach, California.

Rob Staeger lives and writes near Philadelphia. He has written numerous books and stories for young readers, and several plays for older ones.